Sm ckers

Sm♥ches

Kit Whitfield

MQP

Introduction

Do you remember your first kiss?
Do you remember the best kiss you ever had?
The worst?

From ancient times to this very moment, people have
been kissing, in love or in lust: curiously, tenderly,
clumsily, skillfully, gently, or passionately. The simplest of
actions, and yet somehow the most complex, every kiss
is unique: loaded with meaning, a wordless communion
between individual and separate souls. Small wonder that
poets and wits of all ages have loved writing about
kissing more than almost any subject in the world.

This collection is a tribute to the great art of kissing,
and the equally great art of writing. Everyone has
something to say: lovers cajoling their adored objects for
this beautiful favor; moralists issuing grim warnings
about the perilous temptations that flourish when two
people come lip-to-lip; wits casting their bright eyes

over the fumblings and maneuvers or lovers; and poets singing to the glory of it all. There are as many views on kissing as there are kisses and kissers and, whether sharp or sweet, they are notions and comments that we enjoy listening to nearly as much as we enjoy the act itself. Quips and quotes—funny, sensuous, romantic, and charming—are like smooches for our souls and the make us smile, giggle, or sigh.

How many people do you suppose are kissing as you read these words?

We were born to love and long for each other. The strongest and most primal of all impulses is to reach out towards another human spirit. Warm, soft, and intimate: the kiss is the perfect image of, and the loveliest solution to, our deepest needs and wishes. Like humor and kindness, kisses cannot exist in a vacuum, but must be shared. Read on, and take part in the age-old cycle of flirting, laughing, joking, and above all else, kissing, that gives us all that is best and happiest in life.

You are always new.
The last of your kisses
was ever the sweetest…

JOHN KEATS

Partons, dans un baiser, pour
un monde inconnu.

With a kiss let us set out for an
unknown world.

ALFRED DE MUSSET

Hoc osculum mihi
facit bonum apud cor.
Possum volare super tria
clocheria nunc!

This kiss makes me feel
good at heart. I could fly
over three clock-towers now!

GEORGE RUGGLE

Who ran to help me when I fell,
And would some pretty story tell,
Or kiss the place to make it well?
My Mother.

ANN TAYLOR AND JANE TAYLOR

"Watch this." Nancy grabbed the pillow and embraced it. She gave it a long kiss. When she was done she threw the pillow back on the bed. "It's important to experiment, so when the time comes you're all ready. I'm going to be a great kisser some day."

JUDY BLUME

Our little hour—how short it is
  When Love with dew-eyed loveliness
Raises her lips for ours to kiss
  And dies within our first caress.

GEORGE HERBERT CLARKE

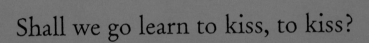

Shall we go learn to kiss, to kiss?

NICHOLAS BRETON

Kisses are the language of
love, so let's talk it over.

AMERICAN PROVERB

Oh, mouth of honey, with
the thyme for fragrance,
Who, with heart in breast,
could deny you love?

SIR SAMUEL FERGUSON

A kiss is the
shortest distance
between the two.

HENRY YOUNGMAN

In the haste of youth we miss
 Its best of blisses:
Sweeter than the stolen kiss
 Are the granted kisses.

EDMUND CLARENCE STEDMAN

It was thy kiss, Love,
that made me immortal.

MARGARET FULLER

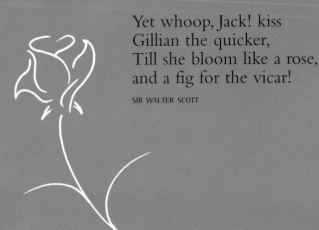

Yet whoop, Jack! kiss
Gillian the quicker,
Till she bloom like a rose,
and a fig for the vicar!

SIR WALTER SCOTT

I love thee like pudding;
if thou wert pie I'd eat thee.

JOHN RAY

The requirements of romantic love are difficult to satisfy in the trunk of a Dodge Dart.

LISA ALTHER

...the kiss...between the mucous membrane of the lips of the two people concerned, is held in high sexual esteem among many nations (including the most highly civilized ones), in spite of the fact that the parts of the body involved do not form part of the sexual apparatus but constitute the entrance to the digestive tract.

SIGMUND FREUD

The mother's first kiss
teaches the child love.

GIUSEPPE MAZZINI

Every maiden's weak
and willin'
When she meets the
proper villain.

CLARENCE DAY

You can't kiss a girl unexpectedly—only sooner than she thought you would.

JACK SEAMAN

A kiss that speaks volumes
is rarely a first edition.

from *A Christmas Cracker*

Something made of nothing,
  tasting very sweet,
A most delicious compound,
  with ingredients complete;
But if, as on occasion, the
  heart and mind are sour,
It has no great significance,
  and loses half its power.

MARY E. BUELL

There's nothing wrong
in a connubial kiss…

LORD BYRON

Our first parents never learn'd to kiss
Till they were exiled from their earlier bowers,
Where all was peace, and innocence, and bliss,
(I wonder how they got through the twelve hours.)

LORD BYRON

Kissing a pretty girl
is like opening a
bottle of olives.
After the first one
the rest come easy.

UNKNOWN

He took the bride about
the neck
And kissed her lips
with such a clamorous
smack
That at the parting all
the church did echo.

WILLIAM SHAKESPEARE

'Tis a secret
Told to the mouth
instead of to the ear.

EDMOND ROSTAND

How about a Spanish kiss under the mistletoe? It's like a French kiss only a little further south.

ANONYMOUS

All of London
littered with
remembered
kisses.

LOUIS MACNEICE

People who throw kisses
are hopelessly lazy.

BOB HOPE

A winning kiss she gave,
A long one, with a free and
yielding lip.

WILLIAM BROWNE

Thou swell! Thou witty!
Thou sweet! Thou grand!
Wouldst kiss me pretty?
Wouldst hold my hand?

LORENZ HART

49

Come, lay thy head
upon my breast,
And I will kiss thee
into rest.

LORD BYRON

You should not take a fellow
   eight years old
And make him swear never to
   kiss the girls.

ROBERT BROWNING

I've been kissin'
Audrey Hepburn
all day and my
pucker is
tuckered.

JAMES GARNER

Rose kissed me today,
  Will she kiss me tomorrow?
Let it be as it may,
Rose kissed me today.

AUSTIN DOBSON

Kisses kept are wasted;
Love is to be tasted.

EDMUND VANCE COOKE

No quarrels,
  murmurs, no delay;
A kiss, a sigh,
  and so away.

RICHARD CRASHAW

A kiss could throw
shivers throughout
her body.

ANAÏS NIN

When caught by his wife,
kissing a chorus girl:
"I wasn't kissing her, I was
whispering in her mouth."

CHICO MARX

Don't look before you leap.
It'll ruin the surprise.

KRIS BRAND

But indeed, dear, these kisses on paper are scarce worth keeping. You gave me one on my neck that night you were in such good-humour, and one on my lips on some forgotten occasion, that I would not part with for a thousand paper ones.

JANE CARLYLE

Amore e'l cor gentil son
una cosa.

Love and the gentle heart
are but a single thing.

DANTE ALIGHIERI

To avoid eye contact, kiss.

MASON COOLEY

May his soul be in heaven—
he deserves it I'm sure—
Who was first the inventor
of kissing.

UNKNOWN

Kisses balmier than half-opening
buds of April.

LORD ALFRED TENNYSON

This gentle beast…
the salt of my cheek
is hers to lick
so long as I
or she shall last…

ADRIAN MITCHELL

[My wife] told me one of the sweetest things one could hear—"I am not jealous. But I am truly sad for all the actresses who embrace you and kiss you while acting, for with them, you are only pretending."

JOSEPH COTTEN

This kiss, the first real one of my life, seemed to me more intimate than anything I'd ever experienced.

ARTHUR GOLDEN

Her lips suck forth my soul.

CHRISTOPHER MARLOWE

A compliment is something
like a kiss through a veil.

VICTOR HUGO

Even birds help
each other. Come
close. Closer.
Help me kiss you.

TESS GALLAGHER

Lean closer, love—I have thy kiss!
Was there another Spring than this?

EDMUND CLARENCE STEDMAN

Kiss—kiss—thou hast won me...

WILLIAM MOTHERWELL

Take me by the earlaps
and match my little lips
to your little lips.

PLAUTUS

My love and I for kisses play'd;
She would keep stakes; I was content;
But when I won, she would be paid;
This made me ask her what she meant.
Pray, since I see (quoth she) your wrangling vain,
Take your own kisses: give me mine again.

WILLIAM STRODE

Never let a fool kiss you,
or a kiss fool you.

JOEY ADAMS

Kisses are like almonds.

SICILIAN PROVERB

Love does on both her lips forever stray;
And sows and reaps a thousand kisses there.

ABRAHAM COWLEY

Only he felt he could no more dissemble,
And kissed her, mouth to mouth,
all in a tremble.

LEIGH HUNT

He kissed me and now
I am someone else.

GABRIELA MISTRAL

A thousand kisses buys
my heart from me.

WILLIAM SHAKESPEARE

Humid seal of soft affections,
  Tenderest pledge of future bliss,
Dearest tie of young connections,
  Love's first snowdrop, virgin kiss!

ROBERT BURNS

Love is the only
game that is not
called on account of
darkness.

ANONYMOUS

Never do with your hands what you could do better with your mouth.

CHERRY VANILLA

Those who can number
their kisses
Will always with few
be content.

C.H. WILLIAMS

Kiss me and take my soul in keeping,
Since I must go, now day is near.

ANONYMOUS

When a clumsy cloud from here meets a fluffy little cloud from there, he billows towards her. She scurries away, and he scuds right up to her. She cries a little, and there you have your shower. They spark. That's the lightning. They kiss. Thunder!

Fred Astaire giving Ginger Rogers an amorous weather report in Mark Sandrich's *Top Hat*

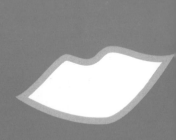

There are as many nuances and inflections
for kisses as there are lips to kiss and
moments in which to bestow them.

TESS GALLAGHER

Tell me who first did kisses suggest?
It was a mouth all glowing and blest;
It kissed and it thought of nothing beside.

HEINRICH HEINE

Strung out and spotty, you wriggle and sigh
and kiss all the fellows and make them all die.

LES MURRAY

…in
An instant's beat
Two souls in flesh confined
May yet in an immortal freedom meet.

WALTER DE LA MARE

A chuck under the chin is worth two kisses.

JONATHAN SWIFT

Her lips are conquerors.

WILLIAM SHAKESPEARE

We turned on one another deep, drowned gazes, and
exchanged a kiss that reduced my bones to rubber
and my brain to gruel

PETER DE VRIES

Who would refuse to kiss a lapdog, if it were preliminary to the lips of his lady?

WILLIAM CONGREVE

There is the kiss of welcome and
of parting, the long, lingering, loving,
present one; the stolen, or the mutual one; the kiss of love, of joy, and
of sorrow; the seal of promise and
receipt of fulfillment.

THOMAS C. HALIBUROTN

I have considered and found
A mouth I cannot leave.

THEODORE ROETHKE

Come back often,
take hold of me in the night
when lips and skin remember...

C.P. CAVAFY

Oh that it were possible
After long grief and pain
To find the arms of my true love
Round me once again!

LORD ALFRED TENNYSON

O let me steal one
liquid kiss,
For Oh! my soul
is parch'd
with love.

ROBERT BURNS

A kiss may ruin
a human life.

OSCAR WILDE

Kisses honeyed by oblivion.

GEORGE ELIOT

Augusta: You have an ant strolling
up your cheek.
Tom: I wish it were your lips.
[She kisses him] Such a little kiss.
Augusta: Such a little ant.
Tom: Wish it had been an elephant.

BILLY WILDER

The moment eternal—just that and no more—
When ecstasy's utmost we clutch at the core
While cheeks burn, arms open, eyes shut, and
    lips meet!

ROBERT BROWNING

Motion can keep me still:
She kissed me out of thought
As a lovely substance will.

THEODORE ROETHKE

Don't have sex man. It leads to kissing
and pretty soon you've got to talk to them.

STEVEN MARTIN

I've always thought of women as kissable, cuddly and smelling good.

State legislator addressing Millicent Fenwick

I kiss you firmly a hundred times...
sketching in my imagination various pictures in
which you and I figure, and nobody and
nothing else.

ANTON CHEKHOV

Here come and sit, where
never serpent hisses;
And being set, I'll smother
thee with kisses.

WILLIAM SHAKESPEARE

Life flowed on
in one eternal kiss.

ELLA WHEELER WILCOX

Have you felt the wool of the beaver,
　　Or swan's down ever?
Or have smelt o' the bud o' the brier,
　　Or the nard in the fire?
　Or have tasted the bag of the bee?
O so white, O so soft, O so sweet is she!

BEN JONSON

Si nám sîn antlüt in ir hende wîz
Únde druhte ez an irmunt, ir wengel klâr:
Owê sô gar wol kuste sîz.

With her fair white hand, she held up the
child's face and pressed it to her mouth and
bright cheeks, and kissed it with sheer delight.

JOHANS HADLOUB

You have absorb'd me.
I have a sensation at the
present moment as though I
was dissolving.

JOHN KEATS

Give me a kiss, add to that kiss a score;
Then to that twenty, add a dozen more:
A thousand to that hundred: so kiss on,
To make that thousand up a million.
Treble that million, and when that is done,
Let's kiss afresh, as when we first begun.

ROBERT HERRICK

Just because I'm sixty-three,
Shall April folly forbidden be?

OGDEN NASH

A tender, sensitive young female tells how she felt when first he kissed her—like a tub of roses swimming in honey, cologne, nutmeg, and blackberries.

S.S. COX

Girl of the red mouth,
Love me! Love me!
Girl of the red mouth,
Love me!

MARTIN MACDERMOTT

A kiss can be a comma,
a question mark or an
exclamation point. That's
basic spelling that every
woman ought to know.

MISTINGUETT

Mayhem, death and arson
Have followed many a thoughtless kiss
Not sanctioned by a parson.

DON MARQUIS

It doesn't matter what you do in the bedroom, as long as you don't do it in the street and frighten the horses.

MRS PATRICK CAMPBELL

Never a lip is curved with pain
That can't be kissed into smiles again.

BRET HARTE

Remember the Viper—
  'twas close at your feet,
How you started and threw
  yourself into my arms;
Not a strawberry there was
  so ripe no so sweet
As the lips that I kiss'd to
  subdue your alarms.

ROBERT BLOOMFIELD

Us kiss and
kiss till us can't
hardly kiss
no more.

ALICE WALKER

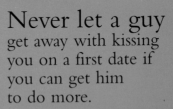

Never let a guy
get away with kissing
you on a first date if
you can get him
to do more.

JOAN RIVERS

When you kiss me, daddy, I stay kissed.

BESSIE SMITH

Nos duo tulla sumus.

We two form a multitude.

OVID

A kiss makes the heart
young again and wipes
out the years.

RUPERT BROOKE

"Kiss" rhymes to
"bliss" in fact as well
as verse.

LORD BYRON

And blessings on the falling out
That all the more endears,
When we fall out with those we love
And kiss again with tears!

LORD ALFRED TENNYSON

The slowest kiss makes too much haste.

THOMAS MIDDLETON

What's in a kiss?
Oh, when for love the kiss is given, this:
Truth, purity, abiding trust, the seal
Of loyalty to love, come woe, come weal,
Unspoken promise a soul's allegiance—this,
All this, and more, ah more! is in a kiss.

MARION PHELPS

We shall want you
and miss you but with
all our might and main
We shall cheer you, thank you, kiss you
When you come back again.

PAUL ALFRED RUBENS

The love that is purest and sweetest
Has a kiss of desire on the lips.

ARTHUR QUILLER-COUCH

What is a kiss? Why this, as some approve:
The sure sweet cement, glue, and lime of love.

ROBERT HERRICK

They heard the wave's splash,
and the wind so low,
And saw each other's dark
eyes darting light
Into each other—and,
beholding this,
Their lips drew near, and
clung into a kiss.

LORD BYRON

[A dog] will kiss the hand that has no food to offer.

GEORGE G. VEST

All really nice girls wonder when men don't try to kiss them. They know they shouldn't want them to and they know they must act insulted if they do, but just the same, they wish the men would try…

MARGARET MITCHELL

I kissed my first
woman and
smoked my first
cigarette on the
same day: I have
never had time for
tobacco since.

ARTURO TOSCANINI

Stolen sweets are
always sweeter,
Stolen kisses much
completer.

LEIGH HUNT

Blush, happy maiden, when you feel
The lips which press love's glowing
   seal;
But as the slow years darklier roll,
Grown wiser, the experienced soul
Will own as dearer far than they
The lips which kiss the tears away.

ELIZABETH AKERS ALLEN

Familiarity breeds attempt.

GOODMAN ACE

What of the soul
was left, I wonder,
when the kissing
had to stop?

ROBERT BROWNING

And in the first
flame
Is all the nectar
of the kiss.

PIGAULT LEBRUN

She took me to her elfin grot,
  And there she wept, and sigh'd
    full sore,
And there I shut her wild, wild eyes
  With kisses four.

JOHN KEATS

Love at the lips was touch
As sweet as I could bear.

ROBERT FROST

O Love, O fire! once he drew
With one long kiss my whole
    soul through
My lips, as sunlight drinketh dew.

LORD ALFRED TENNYSON

They look at each other with their mouths.
They look at each other with their whole bodies.

MURIEL RUKEYSER

...we kiss.
And it feels
like we have
just shrugged
off the world.

JIM SHAHIN

Do me a favor, will you?
Keep away from the windows.
Somebody might ...
blow you a kiss.

A.I. (ALBERT ISAAC) BEZZERIDES

Meet me today! We'll find a wood
Of blackthorn in white bud:
And let me give you one more kiss
Full of sun, free of bitterness.

RICHARD MURPHY

Her neck,
Kissed over close, wears yet a purple
speck
Wherein the pained blood falters and
goes out;
Soft, and stung softly—fairer for a
fleck.

ALGERNON CHARLES SWINBURNE

I kissed you, I own, but I did
   not suppose
That you, through the papers,
   the deed would disclose,
Like free-loving cats, when
   on ridge-poles they meet,
And their squalls of
   "You kissed me!" disturb
   the whole street.

UNKNOWN

Where do the noses go?
I always wondered where
the noses would go.

ERNEST HEMINGWAY

"The sound of a
kiss is not so loud
as that of a cannon,
but its echo lasts a
great deal longer."

OLIVER WENDELL HOLMES

Some women, when
they kiss, blush, some
call the cops, some
swear, some bite, some
laugh, some cry. Me?
I die. Die. I die inside
when you kiss me.

SAMUEL FULLER

Girl, when he gives you kisses twain,
    Use one, and let the other stay;
And hoard it, for moons may die, red fades,
    And you may need a kiss—some day.

RIDGELY TORRENCE

The moth's kiss, first!
Kiss me as if you made believe
You were not sure, this eve,
How my face, your flower,
  had pursed
Its petals up.

ROBERT BROWNING

The decision to kiss for the first time
is the most crucial in any love story.
It changes the relationship of two
people much more strongly than
even the final surrender; because
this kiss already has within it
that surrender.

EMIL LUDWIG

The maiden
who ventures to
kiss a sleeping
man wins of
him a pair
of gloves.

SIR WALTER SCOTT

I will not have my face
smeared with lipstick.
If you want to kiss me,
kiss me on the lips,
which is what a merciful
providence provided
them for.

Herbert Marshall giving Gene Tierney kissing
instructions in Edmund Goulding's *The Razor's Edge*

"May I print a kiss on your lips?" I said,
    And she nodded her full permission;
So we went to press and I rather guess
    We printed a full edition.

JOSEPH LILIENTHAL

There are three
kinds of kisses:
the fire extinguisher,
the mummy and
the vacuum cleaner.

HELEN GURLEY BROWN

Kiss till the cows come home.

BEAUMONT AND FLETCHER

She is such a hot kisser
she melts the gold
in my teeth.

UNKNOWN

I think it is very nice for ladies
   to be lithe and lissome,
But not so much so that you cut
   yourself if you happen to embrace
   or kissome.

OGDEN NASH

Soul meets soul on lovers' lips.

PERCY BYSSHE SHELLEY

Any man who can drive safely
while kissing a pretty girl
is simply not giving the kiss
the attention it deserves.

ANONYMOUS

A kiss, when all is said, what is it?
An oath that's given closer than before;
A promise more precise; the sealing of
Confessions that till then were barely breathed;
A rosy dot placed on the i in loving.

EDMUND ROSTAND

kisses are a better
fate than wisdom

E.E. CUMMINGS

When you kiss me,

jaguars lope through my knees;

when you kiss me, my lips quiver like bronze
violets; oh, when you kiss me.

DIANE ACKERMAN

You can no more keep
a martini in the refrigerator than
you can keep a kiss there.

BERNARD DEVOTO

'Tis but a kiss I beg;
why art thou coy?

WILLIAM SHAKESPEARE

Many a miss would not be a missus
If liquor did not add a spark to her kisses.

E.L.C.

A kiss is now attestedly
a quite innocuous performance,
with nothing very fearful about it
one way or the other.
It even has its pleasant side.

JAMES BRANCH CABELL

I kiss, I feast; but I am hungry still.

ADA CAMBRIDGE

Attentiveness is like kissing—
you can never bestow too
much on your lover.

MICHELLE LOVRIC

Women are a problem, but
they are the kind of problem
I enjoy wrestling with.

WARREN BEATTY

Alcohol is like love.
The first kiss is magic,
the second is intimate,
the third is routine.
After that you take the girl's clothes off.

RAYMOND CHANDLER

"This 'kizz' as you call it is unknown in the west. A rather odd sensation, but one I would not object to repeating. I have an open mind."

You need only open your mouth not your mind, she thought.

TOM ROBBINS

Two people kissing always look like fish.

ANDY WARHOL

A kiss is something you cannot give without taking and cannot take without giving.
ANONYMOUS

Even after the lights had gone up,
while they were shuffling slowly
along the crowd towards the lifts,
its ghost still fluttered against her lips,
still traced fine shuddering roads of anxiety
and pleasure across her skin.

ALDOUS HUXLEY

You are the promised
kiss of springtime that
makes the lonely winter
seem long.

OSCAR HAMMERSTEIN II

Each kiss a heart-quake.

LORD BYRON

I wonder
who's kissing her now.

FRANK ADAMS AND WILL M. HOUGH

A soft lip,
Would tempt you to eternity of kissing!

BEN JONSON

Da mi basia mille, deinde centum,
Dein mille altera.

Give me a thousand kisses,
then a hundred, then a thousand more.

CATULLUS

The first to seize the other's lip
is the winner. As in a game,
it is necessary to take the other
by surprise. Since there is a winner,
a quarrel is inevitable, which is also
a stimulant.

THE KAMA SUTRA

Kiss and be friends.

PETER LANGTOFT

I'm fond of kissing.
It's part of my job.
God sent me down
to kiss a lot of people.

CARRIE FISHER

When I was in pictures, you had a time limit of about two seconds before cutting away to a curtain blowing—and you couldn't open your mouth. If you had a sinus, you'd die.

JOHN DEREK

You kissed me!
   My head drooped low on your breast
With a feeling of shelter and infinite rest,
While the holy emotions my tongue
   dared not speak
Flashed up as a flame from my heart
   to my cheek.

JOSEPHINE SLOCUM HUNT

I love girls who kiss like doves
and hang round my neck.

MARTIAL

Da savium etiam prius quam abis

Give me another naughty, naughty kiss
before we part.

PLAUTUS

I don't know why I should act so experienced.
It's only my second kiss this year.

From *Peyton Place* by Grace Matalious

They are kissing
  to begin the world again.
Nothing
  can stop them.

DORIANNE LAUX

Let thy love and kisses rain
On my lips and eyelids pale.

PERCY BYSSHE SHELLEY

There are swords about me
to keep me safe:
They are the kisses
of your lips.

MARY CAROLYN DAVIES

Touch but my lips with those fair lips of thine…
The kiss shall be thine own as well as mine.

WILLIAM SHAKESPEARE

I can forget my very
existence in a deep
kiss of you.

BYRON CALDWELL SMITH

Shall we kiss? –
My lady laughs,
   delighting in what is.

THEODORE ROETHKE

Anything worth doing well
is worth doing slowly.

GYPSY ROSE LEE

Cats are made for carrying,
For chasing,
Embracing.
Cats are made for carrying,
That's why they're soft, you see.

STEWART COWLEY

A kiss is a lovely trick
designed by nature to stop speech
when words become superfluous.

INGRID BERGMAN

Vex not thy soul with dead philosophy,
Have we not lips to kiss with,
   hearts to love, and eyes to see!

OSCAR WILDE

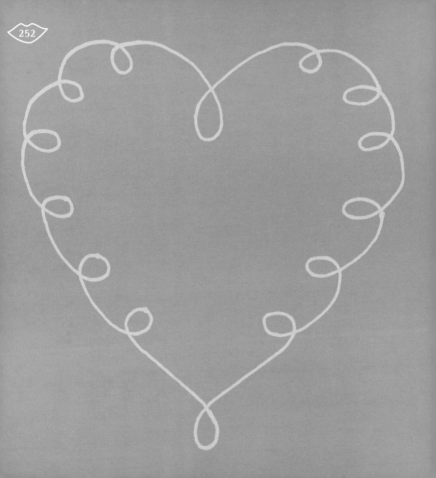

You became so used to the texture and mass of your own tongue that you seldom noticed it. …Having another tongue there felt alien at first, like trying to swallow some small slippery animal, a baby eel or perhaps an energetic oyster.

POPPY Z. BRITE

Kissing is a means of getting two people so close together that they can't see anything wrong with each other.

GENE YASEMAK

Speak, cousin, or if you cannot,
stop his mouth with a kiss.

WILLIAM SHAKESPEARE

It takes a lot of experience
for a girl to kiss like
a beginner.

LADIES HOME JOURNAL

Kissing girls is not like science, nor is it like sport. It is the third thing when you thought there were only two.

TOM STOPPARD

Alas! that women do not know
Kisses make men loath to go.

UNKNOWN

Kiss marks on the ear...are
considered ornamental.

KAMA SUTRA

A lisping lass is
good to kiss.

JOHN RAY

Say I'm weary, say I'm sad,
Say that health and wealth have
  missed me,
Say I'm growing old, but add,
Jenny kissed me.

LEIGH HUNT

The kiss you take is paid
    by that you give:
The joy is mutual, and I'm
    still in debt.

GEORGE GRANVILLE

My lips till then had only known
   The kiss of mother and of sister,
But somehow, full upon her own
   Sweet, rosy, darling mouth—I kissed her.

E.C. STEDMAN

Give yourself a hug—
a big big hug,
And keep on singing,
"Only one in a million
like me
Only one in a million-
billion-thrillion-zillion
like me."

GRACE NICHOLS

He bent her head back across his arm and kissed her, softly at first, and then with a swift gradation of intensity that made her cling to him as the only solid thing in a dizzy swaying world. ...And before a swimming giddiness spun her round and round, she knew she was kissing him back.

MARGARET MITCHELL

If heaven
drops a date, open
your mouth.

CHINESE PROVERB

She swears she's never been
kissed. She can hardly be
blamed for swearing.

UNKNOWN

So sweet love seemed that April morn,
When first we kissed beside the thorn,
So strangely sweet, it was not strange
We thought that love could never change.

ROBERT BRIDGES

I left my love upon the hill, alone,
My last kiss burning on her lovely mouth.

FRANCIS LEDWIDGE

What lies lurk
in kisses.

HEINRICH HEINNE

And when I found your
    flesh did not resist,
It was the living spirit that
    I kissed.

YVOR WINTERS

Whoever named it
necking was a poor
judge of anatomy.

GROUCHO MARX

Kissing…in the old days was very beautiful. Actually the two people doing it were barely touching sometimes, in order to not push her face out of shape. You were doing it for the audience to see what in their minds they always think a kiss is.

RONALD REAGAN

A kiss, and all was said.

VICTOR HUGO

When you tuck me up at night
Stroke my hair and softly hum,
Kiss me and murmur "Sweet, sleep tight!"
Then you're my dearest, bestest Mum.

ANGELA SOMMER–BODENBURG

Gin a body meet a body
Coming through the rye;
Gin a body kiss a body,
Need a body cry?

ROBERT BURNS

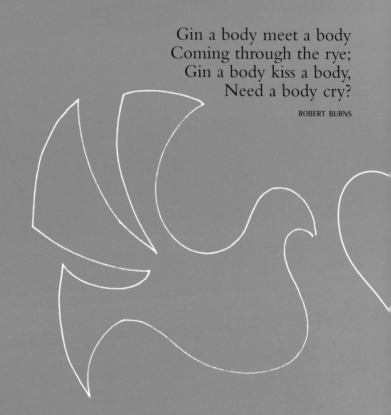

A fine romance with no kisses,
A fine romance, my friend, this is.

DOROTHY FIELDS

Don't make a big exit...
But kiss him quickly,
before you go...

MARLENE DIETRICH

Ruby wasn't particular when she kissed. In fact she led a regular mouth-to-mouth existence.

LILLIAN DAY

Kisses are keys;
wanton kisses are
keys of sin.

JOHN CLARKE

Dame, Amore, besos sin cuento,
Asido de mis cabellos,
Y mil y ciento tras ellos,
Y tras ellos mil y ciento.

Give me, love, innumerable kisses, fast-tied in my
hair, and then eleven hundred more, and then
still eleven hundred more!

CRISTÓBEL DE CASTILLEJO

A kiss without a hug is
like a flower without
the fragrance

MALTESE PROVERB

In Westerns you were
permitted to kiss your
horse but never your girl.

GARY COOPER

His kissing is as full of
sanctity as the touch of
holy bread.

WILLIAM SHAKESPEARE

Do thou snatch treasures
from my lips,
And I'll take kingdoms
back from thine.

R.B. SHERIDAN

How did it happen that
their lips came together?
How does it happen that
birds sing, that snow
melts, that the rose
unfolds, that the
dawn whitens behind
the stark shapes of
trees on the quivering
summit of the hill?

VICTOR HUGO

These poor half-kisses kill me quite.

MICHAEL DRAYTON

Graze on my lips, and when
those mounts are dry,
Stray lower, where the pleasant
fountains lie.

GERVASE MARKHAM AND LEWIS MACHIN

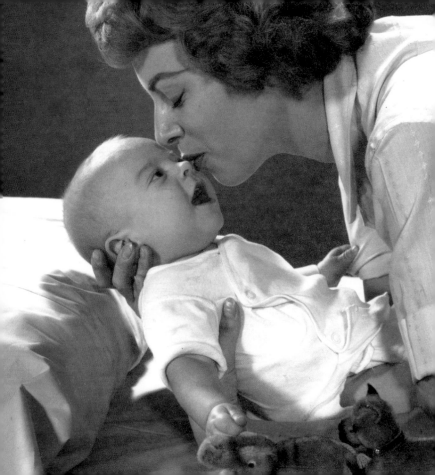

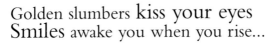

Golden slumbers kiss your eyes
Smiles awake you when you rise...

THOMAS DEKKER

Bachelor's fare; bread and cheese, and kisses.

JONATHAN SWIFT

I fear thy kisses,
  gentle maiden,
Thou needest not
  fear mine.

PERCY BYSSHE SHELLEY

My kisses are his daily feast.

THOMAS LODGE

Fortune shall cull forth
Out of one side her happy minion,
To whom in favour she shall give the day,
And kiss him with a glorious victory.

WILLIAM SHAKESPEARE

Few men know
how to kiss well—
fortunately, I've
always had time to
teach them.

MAE WEST

I have to kiss deeper
and more slowly—your neck,
  your inner arm,
the neat creases under your toes
the shadow behind your knee.

JO SHAPCOTT

Personally, I consider a taxi-cab much more convenient and less expensive than an old-fashioned victoria if you wish to get to some place, but of course guys and dolls engaged in a little offhand guzzling never wish to get any place in particular, or at least not soon.

DAMON RUNYON

One kiss from rosy lips, and
I fear no storm or rock!

OLD GERMAN SONG

The kiss originated
when the first male reptile
licked the first female reptile,
implying in a subtle, complimentary way that she was as
succulent as the small reptile
he had for dinner the
night before.

F. SCOTT FITZGERALD

Give me thy kiss, I'll give it thee again,
And one for interest, if thou wilt have twain.

WILLIAM SHAKESPEARE

My face in thine eye,
mine in thine appears.

JOHN DONNE

Einin kuss in Ehren kann niemand verwehren.

No-one can forbid an honourable kiss.

GERMAN PROVERB

I'll kiss thee yet, yet,
    And I'll kiss thee o'er again,
And I'll kiss thee yet, yet,
    My bonnie Peggy Alison!

ROBERT BURNS

He glared at her a
moment through the
dusk, and the next
instant she felt his arms
about her, and his lips
on her own lips. His
kiss was like a flash
of lightening.

HENRY JAMES

Sweet Helen, make me immortal
with a kiss!

CHRISTOPHER MARLOWE

So sweet a kiss the
golden sun gives not
To those fresh
morning drops
upon the rose.

WILLIAM SHAKESPEARE

She had rather kiss
than spin.

THOMAS FULLER

What is a kiss? Alacke! at worst,
A single Dropp to quench a Thirst,
Tho' oft it prooves, in happie Hour,
The first swete Dropp of our long
   Showre.

CHARLES GODFREY LELAND

A man had given all other bliss,
And all his worldly worth for this,
To waste his whole heart in one kiss
Upon her perfect lips.

LORD ALFRED TENNYSON

Kissing is nigh parent and cousin
unto the foul feat or deed.

WILLIAM CAXTON

The anatomical juxtaposition of two orbicularis oris muscles in a state of contraction.

DR HENRY GIBBONS

Drink to me only with thine eyes,
And I will pledge with mine;
Or leave a kiss but in the cup,
And I'll not look for wine.

BEN JONSON

She allows me to kiss her twice, as though to say,
  "Yes, my entire goodwill is yours, my friend.
  We understand each other: or, at least,
  We strive to make our mutual mystery end."

MARK GIBBON

There's a line between love and
fascination
That's hard to see on an evening
such as this,
For they both give the very same
sensation
When you're lost in the magic
of a kiss.

NED WASHINGTON

Their lips were four red roses on
   a stalk,
Which in their summer beauty
   kiss'ed each other.

WILLIAM SHAKESPEARE

Breath and bloom, shade and shine,—wonder,
wealth,
   and—how far above them—
     Truth, that's brighter than gem,
    Trust, that's purer than pearl—
Brightest truth, purest trust in the universe—
   all were for me
    In the kiss of one girl.

ROBERT BROWNING

Kiss, and cure our quarrel.
Never mind the moral!

HARRIET MONROE

Cana tiene de coles quien besa al hortelano.

She who kisses the market-gardener has a liking for cabbages.

SPANISH PROVERB

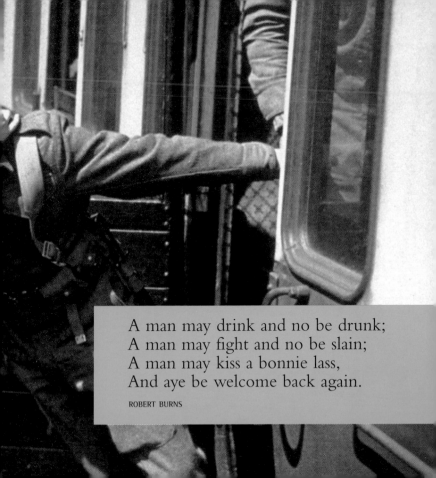

A man may drink and no be drunk;
A man may fight and no be slain;
A man may kiss a bonnie lass,
And aye be welcome back again.

ROBERT BURNS

If your lips itch,
you shall kisse somebody

JOHN MELTON

And then she gave me a sisterly kiss.
Older sister.

NORMAN MAILER

He kissed likewise the maid in the kitchen,
and seemed upon the whole a most loving,
kissing, kind-hearted gentleman.

WILLIAM COWPER

There are certain words of
provocation which men of
honour hold can be properly
answered only by a blow.
Among lovers possibly there
may be some expressions
which can be answered
only by a kiss.

HENRY FIELDING

Where did I first kiss my present
partner? On her insistence.

DAIRE O'BRIEN

Boy: Wow! Where did you learn to kiss like that?
Girl: I used to be a tester in a bubblegum factory.

The Penguin Dictionary of Jokes

He placed his mouth on her
throat, kissing the words
she could not utter.

ANAÏS NIN

[He] kissed her once
by the pigsty when she wasn't looking
and never kissed her again
although she was looking
all the time.

DYLAN THOMAS

Adieux doulx basiers colombins,
Adiux ce qu'en secret faisons
Quand entre nous deux jouons.

Farewell sweet kisses, pigeon-wise,
With lip and tongue; farewell again
The secret sports betwixt us twain.

DIANE DE POITIERS

If…the sunlight clasps the earth
And the moonbeams kiss the sea:
What is all this sweet work worth
    If thou kiss not me?

PERCY BYSSHE SHELLEY

Thy lips, O my spouse, drop as the honeycomb: honey and milk are under thy tongue.

THE SONG OF SOLOMON

In delay there lies no plenty,
Then come kiss me, sweet and twenty.
Youth's a stuff will not endure.

WILLIAM SHAKESPEARE

En fait d'amour, vois-tu, trop n'est pas
même assez.

Where love is concerned, too much is
not even enough!

LE MARIAGE DE FIGARO, P.A.C. DE BEAUMARCHAIS

Anthea bade me tie her shoe;
I did, and kissed her instep too;
And would have kissed unto her knee,
Had not her blush rebuked me.

ROBERT HERRICK

First time he kissed me,
he but only kissed
The fingers of this hand
wherewith I write;
And ever since, it grew
more clean and white.

ELIZABETH BARRETT BROWNING

Sweet red
splendid kissing mouth.

ALGERNON CHARLES SWINBURNE

Kissing was like death from lightning.
If it happened, you didn't know it,
and vice versa.

JESSAMYN WEST

I still remember the chewing gum, tobacco, and beer taste of my first kiss, exactly forty years ago, although I have completely forgotten the face of the American sailor who kissed me.

ISABEL ALLENDE

Never delay kissing a
pretty girl or opening
a bottle of whiskey.

ERNEST HEMINGWAY

Primus titubans audacia furtis.

Sweetest the kiss
that's stolen from weeping maid.

CLAUDIAN

Do not make me kiss,
and you will not make me sin.

H.G. HOHN

She that will kiss, they say,
 will do worse.

ROBERT DAVENPORT

As if he pluck'd up kisses by the roots
That grew upon my lips.

WILLIAM SHAKESPEARE

When the gorse is out of bloom,
kissing's out of fashion.

PROVERB

The musical clink
of tooth against tooth,
the wonderful curiosity
of tongues.

TOM ROBBINS

When two kisses kiss, it's like tigers
answering questions about infinity
with their teeth.

TESS GALLAGHER

I kiss her moving mouth,
Her swart hilarious skin;
She breaks my breath in half;
She frolics like a beast;
And I dance round and round,
A fond and foolish man.

THEODORE ROETHKE

An horse-kiss:
a rude kiss, able to beat one's
teeth out.

JOHN RAY

His mouth is most sweet:
  yea, he is altogether lovely.

THE SONG OF SOLOMON

I dig skin,
lips and
Latin men.

MADONNA

The popular saying is that anyone who kisses the "Blarney stone" will ever after have "a cajoling tongue and the art of flattery or of telling lies with unblushing effrontery".

Lewis's Topographical Dictionary of Ireland

We sing together;
  we sing mouth to mouth.

THEODORE ROETHKE

My kisses
   are his daily feast.

THOMAS LODGE

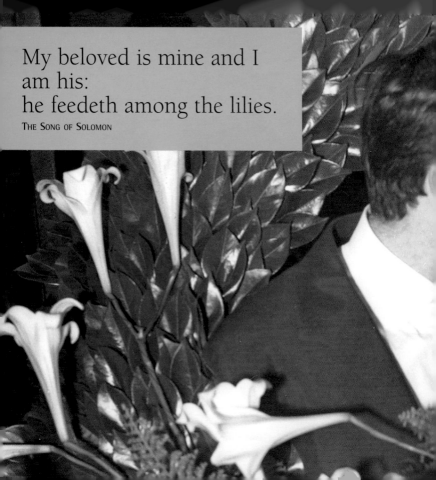

My beloved is mine and I
am his:
he feedeth among the lilies.

THE SONG OF SOLOMON

Says he, "I'd better call agin;"
  Says she, "Think likely, mister!"
Thet last word pricked him like a pin,
  An'…Wal, he up an' kist her.

J.R. LOWELL

He that wipes the child's nose kisses the mother's cheek.

GEORGE HERBERT

"I got a funny sensation in my toes…
like someone was barbecuing them
over a slow flame."
"Let's throw another log on the fire."

TONY CURTIS KISSING MARILYN MONROE, *SOME LIKE IT HOT*

I understand thy kisses and thou mine
And that's a feeling disputation.

WILLIAM SHAKESPEARE

Let him kiss me
with the kisses of his mouth;
for thy love is better
than wine.

THE SONG OF SOLOMON

Master I may be,
But not of my fate.
Now come the kisses, too many too late.
Tell me, O Parcae,
For fain would I know,
Where were these kisses three decades ago?

OGDEN NASH

That girl over there is a fantastic kisser.

How do you know?

I had it from her own lips.

The Penguin Dictionnary of Jokes

…we did one of those
quick, awkward kisses
where each of you gets a
nose in the eye.

CLIVE JAMES

"I've never kissed a woman before."
"Before what?"

JOHN BEAL AND KATHARINE HEPBURN, *THE LITTLE MINISTER*

"I love your hair, your teeth, your lips…"
"Well then, kiss me and stop
taking inventory."

LEOPOLD FECHTNER

Oh, innocent victims of Cupid,
Remember this terse little verse;
To let a fool kiss you is stupid,
To let a kiss fool you is worse.

E.Y. HARBURG

When she lightly kissed me upon my cheek, it felt as though I had been savaged by a frankfurter.

LES DAWSON

A kiss without a moustache
is like an egg without salt.

OLD SPANISH SAYING

It's better to kiss a Miss
than to miss a kiss.

LEOPOLD FECHTNER

Never practice two vices at once.

TALLULAH BANKHEAD

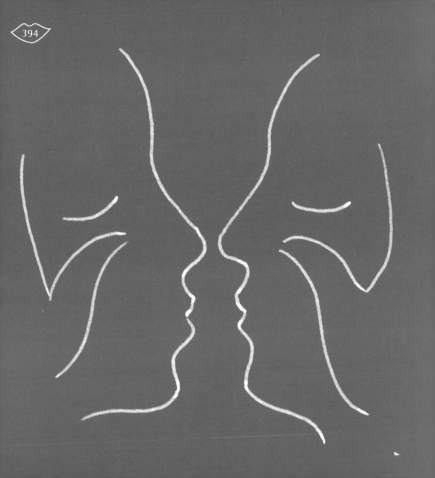

He deposited a kiss further up along her arm, in the nook within the elbow. There the skin was sensitive, and when she folded her arm, it seemed as if the kiss were enclosed and nurtured. Madeleine let it lie there like a preserved flower.

ANAÏS NIN

In love there is always one
who kisses and one
who offers the cheek.

FRENCH PROVERB

Stephen's kiss was lost in jest,
Robin's lost in play,
But the kiss in Colin's eyes
Haunts me night and day.

SARA TEASDALE

After kissing comes
more kindness.

JOHN CLARKE

That little kiss you stole
  held all my heart and soul.

FRANK LOESSER

One kiss
brings honey-dew from
buried days.

JOHN KEATS

In a state of passion,
man and woman suck one another
like lumps of sugar.

KAMA SUTRA

Their souls kissed, they kissed
with their eyes, they were
both but one single kiss.

HEINRICH HEINE

O fie miss,
you must not
kiss and tell.

WILLIAM CONGREVE

Kisses…seem to carry entire worlds.

TESS GALLAGHER

Kissing don't last: cookery do!

GEORGE MEREDITH

Don't throw kisses unless
the girl is a good catch.

UNKNOWN

An' I seed her first a-smokin' of a whackin'
    white cheroot,
An' a-wastin' Christian kisses on an 'eathen idol's
    foot:
        Bloomin' idol made o' mud—
        What they call the Great Gawd Budd—
        Plucky lot she cared for idols when I kissed
        'er where she stud!

RUDYARD KIPLING

Speech happens not to
be his language.

MADAME DE STAËL

I had rather give a
knave a kiss, for once,
than be troubled with him.

JONATHAN SWIFT

When a rogue kisses you,
count your teeth.

HEBREW PROVERB

If love is the
best thing
in life, then
the best
part of love
is the kisses.

THOMAS MANN

If you want to
kiss me any time
during the
evening, Nick,
just let me know
and I'll be glad to
arrange if for you.
Just mention my
name.

F. SCOTT FITZGERALD

A kiss and a drink
o' water make but
a wersh (tasteless)
breakfast.

SCOTTISH PROVERB

Be plain in dress, and sober in your diet;
In short, my deary, kiss me and be quiet.

MARY WORTLEY, LADY MONTAGU

And when my lips meet thine,
Thy very soul is wedded unto mine.

H.H. BOYESEN

But kiss: one kiss! Rubies
unparagoned,
How dearly they do't!

WILLIAM SHAKESPEARE

It is impossible
that this ineffable
kiss does not
cause a tremor
among the stars.

VICTOR HUGO

Forget the moment ere the moment slips,
Kiss with blind lips that seek beyond
    the lips...

RUPERT BROOKE

A kiss is a pleasant reminder that two heads are better than one.

UNKNOWN

When Clark Gable kissed
me, they had to carry me
off the set.

CARROLL BAKER

The kiss. There are all sorts of kisses, lad, from the sticky confection to the kiss of death. Of them all, the kiss of an actress is the most unnerving. How can we tell if she means it or if she's just practicing?

RUTH GORDON

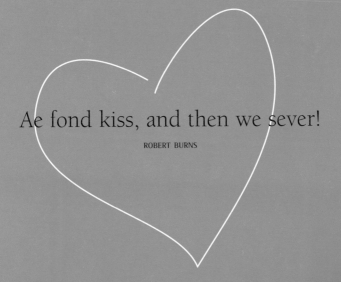

Ae fond kiss, and then we sever!

ROBERT BURNS

There was a curious low roaring sound in her ears as of sea-shells held against them and through the sound she heard the swift thudding of her heart. Her body seemed to melt into his and, for a timeless time, they stood fused together as his lips took hers hungrily as if he could never have enough.

MARGARET MITCHELL

"I saw you take his kiss!" "Tis true."
"O modesty!" "Twas strictly kept:
He thought me asleep;
   at least, I knew
He thought I thought he
   thought I slept."

CONVENTRY PATMORE

"He hasn't actually
kissed me yet, but he steamed
my glasses a couple of times."

LEOPOLD FECHTNER

Kissing your hand may make you feel very, very good but a diamond and saphire bracelet lasts forever.

ANITA LOOS

The seed of desire, born of mutual attraction,
must develop…It must be watered with the
ambrosia of kisses.

THE KAMA SUTRA

I don't think Colin's brother
did very well
at maths or English.
But he got an A*
for snogging.

STEVE TURNER

He drew her into his arms and she
forgot everything but that they had
found each other.

ANTONIA WHITE

Look in mine eyeballs, there
    thy beauty lies;
Then why not lips on lips,
    since eyes in eyes?

WILLIAM SHAKESPEARE

You must remember this,
  a kiss is still a kiss,
A sigh is just a sigh;
The fundamental things apply,
As time goes by.

HERMAN HUPFELD

If only I could seize and hold him
and kiss him as much as I want,
so that I should die of his kisses!

GOETHE

Her ambrosial kiss
That sweeter far than any nectar is.

EDMUND SPENSER

And our lips found ways of speaking
  What words cannot say,
Till a hundred nests gave music,
  And the East was gray.

FREDERIC LAWRENCE KNOWLES

When her loose gown from her
    shoulders did fall,
And she caught me in her arms long
    and small;
Therewith all sweetly did me kiss,
And softly said, "Dear heart, how
    like you this?"

THOMAS WYATT

Come, come, dear Night,
Love's mart of kisses

GEORGE CHAPMAN

For a kiss is an immortal thing.
And the throb wherein those old lips met
Is a living music in us yet.

ROBERT BURNS

Our spirits rushed together
at the touching of our lips.

LORD ALFRED TENNYSON

The universe hangs on a kiss,
exists in the hold of a kiss.

ZALMAN SHNEOR

We kissed…in the garden and this was the best of all with the flowers still expectant in the moonlight and the fragrance of the moist earth and grass rising about us… And it was like sailing from stormy seas into a sweet, safe harbour, like coming home.

JAMES HERRIOT

I was betrothed that day;
I wore a troth-kiss on my lips
I could not give away.

E.B. BROWNING

Maybe the human animal has contributed
really nothing to the universe but kissing and
comedy—but by God that's plenty.

TOM ROBBINS

For love or lust, for good or ill,
Behold the kiss is potent still.

JOHN RICHARD MORELAND

The kiss is melting on my lip—
The last, my love, you gave me;
And dying thus, the doctors say,
Another kiss might save me.

ANONYMOUS

Oh you are a whirlpool,
  you are a whirlpool,
And I am very nearly
drowned.

PAUL DURCAN

Imparadised in one
another's arms.

JOHN MILTON

Text Credits

p.12, Judy Blume, *Are You There God? It's Me, Margaret*, Piccolo, 1980, 1st published in Great Britain in 1978 by Victor Gollancz Ltd, copyright Judy Blume 1970, Pan Books Ltd.

pp.19, 34, 196, 271, 317, 388, 391, 407, 433, from *5,000 One-And-Two Line Jokes: The A–Z of Snappy Sure-Fire Humour On 250 Popular Topics*, ed. Leopold Fechtner, © Parker Publishing Company Inc, 1973.

p.27, 385, from *The Penguin Dictionary of Modern Humorous Quotations*, 2nd edition, ed. Frank Metcalf, 2001.

p.28, from The Stadard Edition of The Complete Psychological Works of Sigmund Freud, Vol. VII, P.150, ed. James Strachey, London, 1953.

p.32, from Clarence Day's, *Thoughts Without Words*, Knopf, New York and London, 1928, imprint of Random House, Inc.

pp.36, 53, 138, 152, from *Stevenson's Book of Quotations, Classical and Modern*, 10th edition, Burton Stevenson, Cassell and Company Ltd, imprint of Cassell and Collier Macmillan Publishers Ltd, London, copyright by Dodd Mead and Company Ltd, 10th edition, 1974.

p.45, Louis MacNeice, "Autumn Journal" from *Collected Poems*, Faber. Used by permission of David Higham Associates.

p.48, "Thou Swell," words by Lorenz Hart, music by Richard

Rodgers © 1927 Harms Inc. USA, Warner/Chappell Music Ltd., London, reproduced by permission of International Music Publications Ltd., all rights reserved.

pp.56, 340, 395, Anais Nin, *Delta of Venus*, Penguin Books, 1st published in Britain by W.H. Allen & Co, 1978, by Penguin 1990, by Penguin Classics 2000, copyright the Anais Nin Trust 1977, p.11.

p.68, Adrian Mitchell, *Don't Go Pet A Porcupine: Poems About Animals*, chosen by and copyright Gervase Phinn, Franklin Watts, London, 2001, p.15.

p.70, from *Memoirs Of A Geisha*, by Arthur Golden, published by Chatto & Windus. Used by permission of The Random House Group Ltd.

pp.73, 96, 365, 405, Tess Gallagher, *Portable Kisses*, Bloodaxe Books, 1992, 1994, 1996 (revised editions).

p.84 (Gabriela Mistral), from *Encarta Book of Quotations: 25,000 Quotations From Around the World*, ed. Bill Swainson, Bloomsbury, 2000.

p.95, 167, 239, from *The Movie Quote Book*, Omnibus Press.

p.98, from *A Gentleman Publisher's Commonplace Book* ed. John G. Murray, 1996, John Murray (Publishers) Ltd.

pp.100, 439, from *The Kiss*, by Walter de la Mare, with permission of the Literary Trustees of Walter de la Mare.

pp.108, 119, 245, 366, 372, Theodore Roethke, *Love's Collected Poems*, Faber and Faber, 1985.

pp.109, 305, from *Hand in Hand: An Anthology of Love poems*, ed. Carol Ann Duffy, Picador, 2001.

p.116, from "Arise My Love, in the forest of Compiegne," by Billy Wilder, *Columbia Encyclopedia*.

pp.135, 197, 382: Ogden Nash, *Candy is Dandy: The Best of Ogden Nash*, selected by Linell Smith and Isabel Eberstadt, Andre Deutsch Ltd, 1994, pp.111–112, 344, 337.

p.143, Alice Walker, *The Color Purple*, The Women's Press Ltd, 1993, copyright Alice Walker 1983.

p.146, from C. Williams and T.W. Waller, *Bessie Smith: The Quintessence; 'The Empress' 1923–33*, Fremeaux & Associates, director Alain Gerber, producer Daniel Nevers.

pp.162, 268, 430, Margaret Mitchell, *Gone With The Wind*, Pan Books, 1st published in Great Britain in 1936 by Macmillan, this edition 1974, pp.303, 519, 817.

p.173, from *The Kiss: A Romantic Treasury of Photographs and Quotes*, Running Press, Philadelphia, London, copyright Running Press 1992.

p.178, from "Sunup", by kind permission of the author and The Gallery Press, Loughcrew, Ireland, from *Collected Poems* (2000).

pp.182, 226, 283, 356, from *The Oxford Dictionary of Phrases, Sayings and Quotations*, ed.

Elizabeth Knowles, Oxford University Press, 1998.

p.205, from *Complete Poems 1904–1962*, by E.E. Cummings, edited by George J. Firmage, by permission of W.W. Norton & Company. Copyright © 1991 by the Trustees for the E.E. Cummings Trust and George James Firmage.

p.207, Diane Ackerman, *Jaguar and Sweet Laughter* copyright © 1991 by Diane Ackerman. Used by permission of Random House, Inc.

p.213, from *10,000 Romantic E-mail Postcards for Him and Her*, ed. Michelle Lovric, Duncan Baird Publishing, 2001, p.25.

p.216: Tom Robbins, *Jitterbug Perfume*, Bantam Books, 2000

p.220, Aldous Huxley, *Brave New World*, Grafton Books, a division of the Collins Publishing Group, London, 1st published in Great Britain by Chatto and Windus, 1932, copyright Mrs Laura Huxley 1932, this edition 1988, p171.

p.222, 326, from *The Oxford Dictionary of Quotations*, revised fourth edition, ed. Angela Partington, Oxford University Press, 1996.

p.223, from *The Wordsworth Dictionary of Film Quotations*, ed. Tony Crawley, Wordsworth Editions Ltd, 1994.

pp.229, 261, 401, 436, *The Complete Kama Sutra: The First Unabridged Modern Translation of the Classic Indian Text*, trs. Alain Danieloh, Park Street Press, Rochester, Vermont, 1994, p.128.

p.240, Dorianne Laux, "Kissing" (excerpt) from *What We Carry*, © 1994 by Dorianne Laux. Reprinted with the permission of BOA Editions, Ltd.

p.248, Steward Cowley, *Little Girls and Boys: Best of Friends*, Deans International Publishing, London, 1986.

p.253, Poppy Z. Brite, (excerpt) from *Drawing Blood*, Penguin, 1994, © Poppy Z. Brite, 1994.

p.258, from *The Invention of Love*, Tom Stoppard, 1997, Grove Press.

p.266, Grace Nichols, *Give Yourself A Hug*, Puffin, 1996.

p.275 (Yvor Winters), (excerpt) "The Marriage" from *Everyman's Pocket Library*, ed. John Hollander, David Campbell Publishers Ltd, 1997. Reprinted from *Collected Poems by Yvor Winters*, with the permission of Carcanet Press Ltd.

p.276, from *Quotations For Our Time*, ed. Dr Lawrence Peter, Magnum Books, 1980, p.462.

p.281, English Version by John Smith from "Ich lieb dich trotzdem immer" © Angela Sommer-Bodenburg.

p.286, from *The New Beacon Book Of Quotations by Women*, ed. Rosalind Maggio, Beacon Press, Boston, 1996, 376:4.

p.310, from *The Crack-Up*, copyright © by New Directions Publishing Corp., with permission.

p.325, from *The Velvet Bow and Other Poems*, Monk Gibbon, published by Hutchinson. Used by permission of The Random House Group Ltd.

p.335, Norman Mailer, *The Deer Park*, © 1955 by Norman Mailer. Used by permission of G.P. Putnam's Sons, a division of Penguin Putnam Inc.

p.341 from *Under Milk Wood*, Dylan Thomas, Everyman, with permission.

p.354, from *Leafy River* by Jessamyn West, © 1967 Jessamyn West and renewed 1995 by Ann Cash and Harry M. McPherson, reproduced by permission from Harcourt, Inc.

pp.364, 454, Tom Robbins, *Even Cowgirls Get The Blues*, Bantam Books, 1995, © Tom Robbins, 1976.

p.385, from *The Penguin Dictionary of Modern Humorous Quotations*, ed. Frank Metcalf, Penguin, 2001, p.169.

p.389, E.Y. Harburg, *Inscriptions On a Lipstick*, reprinted with the permission of The Harburg Foundation.

p.390 (Les Dawson), from *Harrap's Book of Humorous Quotations*, ed. G.F. Lamb, Harrap Books Ltd, 1996. Excerpt taken from Les Dawson's *The Amy Pluckett Letters*, Robson Books, 1982. Reprinted with the permission of Chrysalis Books Ltd.

p.414, from *The Oxford Dictionary of Thematic Quotations*, OUP, 2000.

p.416, Reprinted with permission of Scribner, an imprint of Simon

& Schuster Adult Publishing Group, from *The Great Gatsby* by F. Scott Fitzgerald. Copyright 1925 by Charles Scribner's Sons. Copyright renewed 1953 by Frances Scott Fitzgerald Lanahan.

p.434, from *The New Penguin Dictionary of Quotations*, ed. J.M. and M.J. Cohen, 1st published 1960, this edition 1998.

p.437, *Dad, You're Not Funny* by Steve Turner, published by Lion Publishing PLC, 1999. Copyright © Steve Turner.

p.400 (Frank Loesser) from *The Columbia World of Quotations*, Ed. Robert Andrews *et al.* Columbia University Press, 1996, nos. 40953, 36652.

p.444, from *Remembered Kisses: An Illustrated Anthology of Irish Love Poetry*, ed. Fleur Robertson, Gill and Macmillan Ltd, 1996, p78.

p.449, Zalman Shneor, *The Little Book of Love*, Penguin, 1997.

p.450, James Herriot, *Let Sleeping Vets Lie*, Pan Books, 1974 with the permission of David Higham Associates.

Picture Credits

Published by MQ Publications Limited
12 The Ivories, 6–8 Northampton Street, London N1 2HY
Tel: 020 7359 2244   Fax: 020 7359 1616

Copyright © MQ Publications Limited 2002

Design: Bet Ayer
Text compiled by: Kit Whitfield

ISBN: 1–84072–464–1

Printed and bound in France by Clerc s.a.